A Little Light from the Borders

Poems after Ezra Pound

Edited by
Jeff Grieneisen
and Rhett Forman

II

The Ezra Pound Center for Literature

The Ezra Pound Center for Literature Book Series is a project dedicated to publishing a variety of scholarly and literary works relevant to Ezra Pound and Modernism, including new critical monographs on Pound and/or other Modernists, scholarly studies related to Pound and his legacy, edited collections of essays, volumes of original poetry, reissued books of importance to Pound scholarship, translations, and other works.

Series Editor: John Gery, University of New Orleans

Editorial Advisory Board
Barry Ahearn (Emeritus), Tulane University
Massimo Bacigalupo (Emeritus), University of Genoa
Ronald Bush (Emeritus), University of Oxford
Peter Liebregts, University of Leiden
A. David Moody (Emeritus), University of York
Ira B. Nadel, University of British Columbia
Tim Redman, University of Texas at Dallas
Richard Sieburth, New York University
Demetres Tryphonopoulos, University of Alberta, Augustana Campus

Also Available in the Ezra Pound Center for Literature Book Series

John Gery, Daniel Kempton, and H. R. Stoneback, Editors,
 Imagism: Essays on Its Initiation, Impact and Influence. Introduction by Helen Carr.
Catherine E. Paul,
 Fascist Directive: Ezra Pound and Italian Cultural Nationalism
Anderson Araujo,
 A Companion to Ezra Pound's Guide to Kulchur
Richard Parker, Editor,
 Readings in The Cantos, Volume 1 and Volume 2
Catherine Paul and Justin Kishbaugh, Editors,
 A Packet of Poems for Ezra Pound
Justin Kishbaugh and Catherine E. Paul, Editors,
 Ezra's Book
Massimo Bacigalupo,
 Ezra Pound, Italy, and The Cantos
John Gery, Walter Baumann, and David McKnight, Editors,
 Cross-Cultural Ezra Pound
John Gery and Viorica Patea, Editors,
 Song Up Out of Spain: Poems in Tribute to Ezra Pound
Viorica Patea, John Gery, and Walter Baumann, Editors,
 Ezra Pound and the Spanish World
Anderson Araujo and Ronald Bush, Editors,
 The Pound Biennial, Volume 1

A Little Light from the Borders

Poems after Ezra Pound

Edited by
Jeff Grieneisen
and Rhett Forman

© 2025 Clemson University
All rights reserved

First Edition, 2025

ISBN: 978-1-63804-193-1

© 2025 Jeff Grieneisen and Rhett Forman
(editorial matter and arrangement)

The copyright of individual contributions remains with the authors.

Cover design by Mars O'Keefe

To order copies, please visit the Clemson University Press website:
www.clemson.edu/press/

Acknowledgments

The editors would like to thank John Gery for his invaluable advice and direction as we navigated the intricacies of assembling this volume of poems. We would also like to thank the de Rachewiltz family members for their continued support and assistance with Pound studies and especially for opening their home so that we might gather to celebrate Mary's 100th birthday with a conference in honor of her father. We are also indebted to Alison Mero, Andrew Dorkin, and Gloria J. Aragon at Clemson University Press for their work on the design and publishing side, and to *The Kenyon Review*, where the poem 月 by Chengu He 何琤茹 first appeared (reprinted here by permission).

Introduction

by Jeff Grieneisen and Rhett Forman

We have made new a line from Canto 92 of *Rock-Drill* as the title for the fifth poetry anthology to arise from the Ezra Pound International Conference (EPIC):

> 2 thousand years, desensitization
> After Apollonius, desensitization
>   & a little light from the borders:
>   Erigena,
>   Avicenna, Richardus. (92/642)

In its immediate context, this "little light" refers to the splendor of paradise emerging along the fringes of an otherwise dark human history. This history records how humanity has abandoned its most beautiful and redeeming ideas, artwork, and "sacraments" (92/641) in exchange for quick wealth, cheap comforts, and divisive political power. With our volume, however, we hope for a different kind of exchange, one which unifies instead of divides. While respecting the borders between people that lend richness to local time and place, we intend this anthology to give each of its authors and readers an experience of the light "and as engraven on gold, to be unity" (92/638). We also cannot help but recall from the word "borders" the borderland of the nation that hosted the 30th EPIC: Scotland. For us, the border serves as the negative space, no less necessary for being void, out of which the light that unites must radiate.

Pound scholarship offers a forum for such an exchange across the bounds of language, political situations, and continents. EPIC serves as the ongoing legacy of a poet who strove to make the most redeeming ideas and images cohere, and the poetry anthologies that have arisen from the conference have extended this legacy into the twenty-first century. Since 2018, Clemson University Press has published these anthologies in connection with the conferences at Brunnenburg Castle, Italy (2017; edited by Catherine Paul and Justin Kishbaugh), the University of Pennsylvania (2019; edited by Justin Kishbaugh and Catherine Paul), and the University of Salamanca, Spain (2019; edited by John Gery and Viorica Patea). In addition, the COVID-era 2022 online conference hosted by Japanese Poundians produced an independently-published, bilingual volume edited by Miho Takahashi. We are pleased that Clemson University Press, Alison Mero, and John Gery are once again bringing to readers an important collection of contemporary poetry in the tradition of Pound as part of the Ezra Pound Center for Literature Series.

The struggle to define and transcend borders resonates with the work of each poet in this collection, as do Pound's wide-ranging interests. The translations of Japanese poet Kenji Miyazawa (1896-1933) by Hidetoshi Tomiyama and Michael Pronko express a longing for light and the divine on the threshold between life and death, while bilingual poet Chengru He meditates on reflected moonlight and the correspondence of image and thing after Pound's ideogrammic method. John Gery and Justin Kishbaugh retreat into the surety of the image and provide formal grounding where rhythm instantiates an exploration of memory and the difficulty of pinning down existence. Biljana Obradović's and Jeff Grieneisen's works are both highly personal and cosmopolitan, celebrating the mundane in extraordinary places and employing colloquial language to fashion acute imagist studies. Likewise, Matz McLaughlin's multi-lingual collages, blues rhythms, and haiku adapt the finest qualities from world literature. Mary Maxwell and Silvia Falsaperla remake myths and ancient heroines, mixing travel poetry with Homeric echoes. Stephen Romer and Ron Smith revisit modernist moments, Romer with satire on current sensitivities and a reversal of the elite and vulgar, Smith with an ekphrastic sequence tracing Pound's life in pictures. Tony Lopez and Rhett Forman deliver precision in time and place, the former studying intellectual and linguistic borders, the latter the American frontier and its dialects. Each poet in the collection resides on the precarious edge between the personal and the universal.

Four poems by Mary de Rachewiltz serve as the "adjunct to the Muses' diadem" (*Mauberley*) included in this anthology. Her *ars poetica* "A Poet Is What the Poet Is" initiates readers into the holy mystery of memory, while in "The Cloak She Wears Is Solitude" we find the projection of the past onto natural accidents. "Each Step Tells Another Story" displays a clash of narratives interrupting each other, transgressing boundaries until the heaviest of objects becomes the source of light—both levity and brilliance. Finally, "Cultur" plays on the origin of *culture* in agrarian cultivation, illuminating the consistent process underlying good agriculture, art, and humanity. Throughout, de Rachewiltz makes the whole cohere across borders without dissolving beautiful particulars.

As we cross another barrier into the future of Pound studies, we believe this volume will convince readers of Pound's importance for world literature. Even now while compiling this, we are preparing for the 31st EPIC at Brunnenburg where we will look at the poet's past to carry forward his sometimes splendid and sometime frustrated attempts to bring the best human ideas and images into conversation in the hope that what we all "lovest well remains" (81/540).

Mary de Rachewiltz

"A Poet Is What the Poet Is"

1

A Poet is what the poet is
in the eyes of the beholder.
A Poem is what the poem does
in the mind of the reader.
Imagination forms a figure
alive in the air.
      It's the soul that cuts
a form in outer space
the sensitive heart apprehends
though none knows
where a soul begins or ends,
created as we are
         after His own Image.

Reality lies between the alive
and the re-lived unendingly.

2

Did Marianne M. ever consider
the nymphalid ground plan
with its potential of 100,000
variants and talk with Plotinus
about the creation
         of a yellow butterfly?
Colors are to the mind
an elixir, they quicken the senses —
infinite hues in the sky follow
the clouds and the green gray blue ripples
of the sea on the white foam.
Can you tell me what happens
         to the memory of colors?
The tiny yellow squares on a mauve apron

my nurse wore vivid
as the tiny yellow flowers
in a meadow of later years. Yellow is
the first color I mastered,
its glitter called as gold to a magpie.
Tiny details told a story
to the retina of a child's eye
and gave her a voice
    "well worn from poetry."

3

Of the myriad that died
lovers in throngs now claim life
in the hearts of their women
for generations to come
    and bring peace.
The cat on my lap was a panther
of old under the rose bush
waiting for sunrise and the lion
to fight and destroy unto death.
In their ashes the dove-turtles coo
monotonously.
    I keep the cat
behind closed windows lest the birds
and the squirrels, though swift and small,
fall prey to a dreaming survivor:
dearest, I owe you a monument.

4

I.
Many fall by the roadside
the address leads them astray;
unheeding the call of con-
vention, they sit in dark pubs,
heads drooping, glass in hand says:
"bottoms-up," while they sink
amid ashes and sawdust
to the bottom, so young.

II
Passports and pacemakers in old age
have to be renewed or changed only
every ten or fifteen years, you said —
yet I was unable to live with
an electric heart ticking away
as did once Father Chronos,
so cruelly I allowed you
to go Sterling Emeritus and die alone
    in a posh day-care-center.

5

I dreamt I stole a little fish,
the little fish was you, I know,
you beckoned on an unguarded
shelf and came unstuck easily
from your pedestal,
pale and smooth in my hand,
an onyx perhaps, an ancient
Egyptian artifact.
I knew I stole you and others
might be blamed if found
among my amulets.

Fearfully blissful I awoke,
hands joined in my crotch,
thinking of the Saint that swooned.

6

How would I know so & so
is right when describing a bee
or a cow calving,
had I not seen the bare arm
pulling out a slimy head
or a man and a woman pulling
at the legs with a rope
for a new creature to glide over clean straw.

To few it has been given
to see such things in a warm stable
and believe that a solitary man
plays the accordion
to commune with beasts — as I have read.

A writer's best friend is aloneness:
no creativity course can substitute
what in dark old age memory
pulls from a primordial
holy cow's womb and know-how,
with elbow-grease sharpen
the pencil ready to write.

2000-2005

"The Cloak She Wears Is Solitude"

The cloak she wears is Solitude;
the flock that gave the wool for it
no longer grazes in her field.
The whir of the spinning wheel died
long ago, the clack of the loom
has been hushed. She walks with Silence,
her best friend, while gray-brown leaves
rustle under her feet; their hues
recall the colors of her sheep:
white, black, brown, that gave the strong thread
to protect her from wind and rain
that neither fades in glaring sun
nor offends the whiteness of the snow:
Nature provides her fashion show.

        p.s. for P.M.'s: *remoteness*.
        Alonitude is a better word
        to wear as a cloak
                and silence
        she may substitute with
                God's Voice.

2006

"Each Step Tells Another Story"

Each step tells another story.
In a stone language never known
you hear the sounds
of a denary scale: do re
mi fa — *ut* is the pattern in
the ripple of the waves in gray
if ascending into blackness.

Going down the long path to the green
where two birch trees
tell the story of another
era in a silver-lined speech
you hear: *Right* is
the Law we can't fathom, the light
in the stone beyond nature's chrome.

The load is heavy and lives in
the weight of the loss we carry.
Stone alone is free
of guilt-breeding
                passion.

Cultur

If from the one to the few
and from the few to the many
kindness flows, it will be as if
a soft wind were bringing seed
          to a barren ground.
From the kernel in the grape-
pulp up shoots the vine and
from one grain the ear of wheat.
The vineyard and the five-grain-field
give bread and wine to the many.

Green moss grows on a flat roof,
lichens and morning glory
among tufts of spring onion
brought by Scirocco winds
or dropped from bird's beak.

So could the world grow green
if kindness from the one
to the few and from the few
to the many were to spread
not as a replica incarnate:
Art into agri-
         culture.

Silvia Falsaperla

Aerial Odyssey Interrupted

for Galateia Demetriou

Odysseus' journey
was sea-swept and wind-beaten
sighting land
in periplum.
In an airplane
10,000 feet above the Ionian Sea
I look down from my window seat
sighting Aci Trezza on the east coast
of three-legged Sikelia

I see Aci shepherd in a greeny field
beloved of Galatea sea nymph
Galatea beloved of Aci
Galatea beloved of Polyphemus
the Cyclops
goat-smelly but harbouring tender feelings
his one eye big enough to see Aci and Galatea
embrace in the bushes
and in a raptus flung a boulder rock
and crushed Aci dead.
Galatea turned Aci into a river
water element just like her
and together they flow into the sea every day
for lovers to swim out and merge in the waters
of enduring love

Polyphemus threw rocks at Odysseus too,
foreigner, liar, jokester
calling himself Nobody when he blinded
forlorn, love-lorn Polyphemus to get his last laugh—
"Tell them nobody blinded you!"
The two lava rocks are still there
close to shore like two

rough-edged, cone-shaped *arancini* rice balls
I swam as a dolphin
I swam as a nereid in the waters of endless love for Aci and Galateia
I know Scylla and Charybdis
are lurking, hiding in the depths
besetting the narrow strait of Messina
golden Zancle
with ten-headed waves and a swallowing whirlpool
The airship
my steady bird of steel
gliding over
the Aeolian islands
map-perfect from my realm of rarified air
cloud-clear
isles wind-locked and windswept
by windy Aeolus
Vulcano looking up, its savage crater
o-mouth of fire
islands sputtered out
from the roiling depths
Alicudi, Filicudi, nearby Salina
of the once-salty lake

Tracking my great-uncle Odysseus
Ulysses! to my Romanized lips
my wily hero ancestor
striving towards Ithaca and Penelope
to primal home and love
O me the gods!
—the islands and sea now recede over land—
my 21st century sleek metal bird ship
flies me off course
with its metal wings and motors
inexorably north to Rome—not east to Corfu,
once Kerkyra, to gentle Nausicaa saving
Odysseus naked on shore like his men from shipwreck

---

arancini - (It.) Sicilian rice balls stuffed with cheese and other ingredients

Odysseus' unsullied love for Nausicaa
Nausicaa's providential love, not the heady lotuses
men-dooming Circe and Calypso;
but with new ship and new men returning
to Ithaki and Penelope
abiding love knitting the years

O metal bird, fly me back, fly me south!
Let me return to three-legged Sikelia
of the medusa face on the flag
for my journey of ancient love and lore
isn't yet over
Persephone beloved of Hades
Persephone beloved of Demeter
Demeter beloved of Persephone
all begetting winter, spring, summer, and fall.

chiaroscuro

in deep caverns
Demeter nude
with raw desire
lay in bed with dead king
Thanatos
to unite with him

the images of sleep
lend clarity
to conscious day
and unite in the folds
of night streams

mater, you are home
light greets me
the floor is a mosaic
of blue and topaz blooms
and the billowing curtains
diffuse sunlight

and the rooms each
with bowls of flowers
Venus
of springtime
blows flowers
from her mouth

The Garden of Kolymbethra

Down the path is the garden—
past the ridge of temples of the gods.
We've have been away from Akragas for long—
wind-flung, unclaimed
children of Megali Ellada.
The trees are silent and fruit bearing
—mandarins, chinotti, and bergamots.
They provide shade in the midday heat.
I chance upon a mulberry tree—
I know its delights from a memory of youth.
I reach up and pluck the berries
one by one; god-sweet, ambrosial;
I eat where the gods feast every waning sun.
The blood-purple juice stains me—mouth,
hands, my robe of mottled orange, yellow, and green.
In a rapture spell the tree takes me in—
My body merges with the trunk,
my hands spread branches,
my feet run roots,
my lips drip black-red mulberries.
I have come home
to my family of olive-toned gods,
begot by them,
my face a transfixed glow.
— Dryad!

Now you, *kouros*, finding wild
capers growing in the parched soil,
pick a lime
and be a lime tree among us
water-gushed
by the nearby Moorish pool.

RHETT FORMAN

The Fable of the Onion

brother beat the black roller down to Odessa
and hunkered in the *dusty old dust*
with a Tamaulipan ranchero up from Reynosa—
they ate tamales and some kind of menudo

the man put to him a fable he heard of old—
a widow of Laredo whose breath
befouled the earth died and was took up
by the river they call the Phlegethon
and here her angel found her and asked God
to spare her and He asked if she had done
just one good work just one and the angel said
she gave an onion once to a beggar
out on the bridge to Matamoros
a sweet onion from Laredo grown on the rio
and so for the sake of that onion
let her enter the gates and the Lord said
if you can take that onion and pull her
from the Phlegethon then it is so and the angel
went straightaway and the onion held firm
but when the souls of the damned began
to clamor out on her back she rebuked them
saying she alone and not they may swim ashore
and at that moment the onion grown away off
in the border country down on the Rio Grande
where the jaguarundi stalks in the reeds
blew out like an oilwell sparking hellfire on the basin

Dust Bowl Blues for the End Times

Palm Sunday, April 14, 1935

hush up mama hush up hush up
hush up mama mama
hush up mama hush up hush up
hush up mama hush up

boy down Lubbock sung some new blue tune
dust billowed up like linen
dust come up like blood I tell ya

at dawn Jesus rode in on an ass
by afternoon Famine on a black steed

bear witness said the sermoner John and James go on and fetch me that foal
bear witness said the sermoner the quiet death in black corners
and nothing but windrattle and sandfall like light through eaves

hush up mama hush up hush up
hush up mama mama
hush up mama hush up hush up
hush up mama hush up

it was—she said—it were the end—
said it were the end of the world
I believed her surely I did

Guthrie Sings the Hymn of the Dead

I am Lazarus rose from the dead
only to die another time again

the dust rose up like locusts of Moses
come up like locusts of Moses I tell ya
the dust sang down like cicada rattles in June
the dust on your plate like chicken flour
the dust on the back of the calico cat
the dust mowed crop like a reaper
the dust come down like Junior clubbing the jackrabbits
the dust come up soft and distant like mother song
the dust high like choirs of angels
and the seraphim flapping mightily

the dust come knocking like the banker
the dust come knocking like the mortgage broker
the dust come knocking like the debt collector
the dust come knocking like the tractor lender
the dust come knocking like the tax man
the dust come knocking like the deputy and the sheriff and all them boys
come knocking like them what live off you until you die

the dust a god's vengeance for forgetting
the responsibility of the impious and unprepared
dust come down like Roman law like moans of lepers
the dust settles like the Galilean at the table where Levi sat
the dust settles like you when you give up the ghost
the world an empty tomb after the dust cloud
all that silent reckoning
the dust rose up like lungs of Lazarus
the dust died—died again like Righteous Lazarus the Four Days Dead

and for the rest of his thirty years which he spent as Bishop in Cyprus he did not smile
for all the woe he had witnessed in the underworld but one day in the port
of Levantine waters he saw a thief take an earthen pot and laughed—the dust steals
the dust

John Gery

Salisbury Crag at Twilight

As seen from the Burns Monument, Edinburgh

A giant's head reclined, not
        dead, eyes gazing at the sky,
gaunt-faced, the small patch of trees
        lining his lip to the west
his mustache no less, on this
        side (the north) his beard growing
sideburns, his ear the descent
        by Holyrood Park. At dusk,
whether under cloud cover
        or not, there's plenty to keep
his drowsy Majesty a-
        wake — until the stars arouse
bright city lights on his chest!

Not so rough, his raised brow seems
        here from across the bog by
Bobbie Burns, his monument —
        stone cage without Burns in it —
where it's easy to declare,
        whether to air or to those
who may or may not care, how
        tough it can be to survive,
not easy to lie nor lie
        back (with words in his body
and his body on its back),
    silent, deliberately
clenching teeth, his upper lip
        and the cower of his frown
crossing north to south on ground
        part lopped and part lopsided.
Does he not want a whiskey,
        this browsing gentleman, he

who, shaded in silhouette,
                seems temporarily wise,
his nose squared as Arthur's Seat,
                so radically huge, so sweet?

Daft Draft

This open window blows no
    ill-willed wind in, though
the motive someone must have

had to have left it half-open
    will no doubt remain forever
questionable — as for those ducks

who turn angel food cake
    down in City Park, then peck
at paper stuck in their poop.

Who knows why I, for
    instance, ever thought
my idea for love would fly,

or how I ever knew the girl
    just for me would never see
me for her, those white bucks

I begged for in my head
    instead making the man
I later came to hate ridiculous

right before he was dead?
    Even to ask you
here and now to forgive me

seems daft — not because
    like a coalminer after
a double shift underground

I don't deserve
    your kindness, despite
my sullying the world

for a living, but for whatever
    virtue in me you may not wish
to acknowledge, as though one

small gesture might instead gestate
    explosive love. But
I'm not thinking of that today,

only this breeze, hoping it
    will eventually please
even you, with or without me.

The Long Lost One

It has no borders, time, no gate
    to walk through, latch, or lock.
I thought, maybe, I could create
    from missing you a block,

a back door I might soon learn not
    to open. I believed
in fading, in the mood distraught
    diminished by my need

to move on, though not through a door
    but toward insensate things –
the norm of numb, those days before
    punched by a white joy that sings.

How wrong! The further you're removed
    the likelier you'll stay,
like slashes cut in marble grooved
    scored permanently gray.

Heretofore

We didn't talk enough; we talked too much.
The drift swirled by the window. Later on
when one of us paused to check on the snow,
he said, *I can't see anything out there*

(the night had fallen), *nothing*. Soon years passed
and still we hadn't talked enough. I asked
offhand, one day, what had happened to him
I'd known once, him I had not known I had

not known. As though some sudden noise, a train horn
or flock of birds rising had blocked my voice,
she wiped the sponge across another plate
and stacked it prudently. I stepped aside

to watch the twilight through the door, the screen
grey, with a few flies. Like those other times
again politely I ignored the quiet,
though this time I could see that she was thinking,

thinking of him. Too much I'll never tell;
too much of her life she has kept from me,
not secretly, just unaccounted for.
I've talked too much, not knowing heretofore

I've never talked enough; I've thought too much
of her, of him, of flies, the small hairbrush
another smoothed her hair with late one night
when last we met at her airport hotel,

after which I can't say. When I fall ill,
maybe she'll ask. Or like those other times
maybe she'll think, what does it matter now?—
he's dying. Or maybe the world will change.

Standing in Old Age

The crooked part when I sit,
lap extended like a leaf
for a tray across my thighs,
my back racked up, if I fit
well, head held high like a cliff
from which hair and tears fall, sighs

expiring, until I rise -
or have to rise - beleaguered
by what has driven me to
drop here, with my bloodshot eyes,
the rough grid rig that triggered,
suddenly, exhaustion: Who

pared me to pieces? Who said,
*Now that you've stood this long, bend
like a tree from rain*? Age fills,
then kills, rigid in your head,
the speed you hope will extend
indefinitely. Yet love, too, spills

indiscriminately through
not just from *you* but from those
you've loved, the living or dead,
even - a miracle, too,
standing, sitting, lying in bed,
how the rain opens a rose.

Jeff Grieneisen

Where I Notice It

Parentheses
around the mouth,
those lines
that weren't there
show through
slow chewing.

Something's missing,

some heft
over top teeth,
some matter
around cheekbones
now so well defined,

something in the eyes
pleading
with time,
destiny,
a glimmer
dimmed into fear.

Slowly resigned
to small food,
quiet walks
to the bathroom,
running a finger
over the ridges
of a thin face
in an unfamiliar mirror.

Erosion takes
the subtle fatty layers
and
eventually
leaves
nothing.

In Lierna

We sit amid this after-work crowd,
drafts pulled hastily into glasses,
burnt pizza carried to our table.

Ruffians drink small beers,
bar maid shoos flies off tapas
with an old fly swatter,
sometimes knocks the ham
from thin bread,
and puts it back
without shame.

Contents

Acknowledgements

Introduction   IX

Mary de Rachewiltz   1
     "A Poet Is What the Poet Is"
     "The Cloak She Wears Is Solitude"
     "Each Step Tells Another Story"
     Cultur

Silvia Falsaperla   8
     Aerial Odyssey Interrupted (for Galateia Demetriou)
     chiaroscuro
     The Garden of Kolymbethra

Rhett Forman   13
     The Fable of the Onion
     Dust Bowl Blues for the End Times
     Guthrie Sings the Hymn of the Dead

John Gery   16
     Salisbury Crag at Twilight
     Daft Draft
     The Long Lost One
     Heretofore
     Standing in Old Age

Jeff Grieneisen   23
     Where I Notice It
     In Lierna
     After Postmodern Question

Chengru He 何琤茹   26
     月

Justin Kishbaugh — 30
   Three from Three Squared

Tony Lopez — 32
   Cartesian Light
   In the Air
   Meaning Empty

Mary Maxwell — 37
   Boudicca in the Underworld

Matz McLaughlin — 39
   Après Villon
   Old Panther (For Ezra Pound)
   Three Seasons Haiku

Biljana D. Obradović — 43
   Lost Loot Value
   My Yoga Class
   Symmetry
   The Mask: Il Dottore, Il Medico Della Peste
   Greek Island Vacation

Kenji Miyazawa — 50
   translated by Hidetoshi Tomiyama and Michael Pronko
   The Spirit Song
   Untitled
   Untitled

Stephen Romer — 53
   A Set of Satirical Verses (In Honour of EP)

Ron Smith — 57
   Album (15 poem series)

Contributors — 63

After Postmodern Question

White smoke rises
from butt-ends of Marlboros,
one left-over oyster cracker
limps in humid air,
a pinned insect
scratches the balsa wood floor
in the cigar box.

I fashion myself a prude
against the swelling sea of voices
wandering through Wal-Mart
aisles at 11 p.m. or 1 a.m.
I wonder when my head will be served up,
when I'll learn to ask the questions
that need to be asked.

Before they choose the carts,
load the merchandise
of one-night-only cheap-stuff racks,
there is smoke
rising into drifts
like evaporating wreaths,

scattering into the questions
we all have, overwhelming questions
that lead us to new leaders,
frightening mirrors
against which we appear silent.

Chengru He 何琤茹

月

"月" is published on The Kenyon Review, spring 2024.

(a)

there is always a waxing crescent in poetry

                            between the new moon and full phase
                rising   hanging itself
                        on top
                of a pine

        a smiling eye
looking West   blinking   measuring
                      time with her shadow

            first   a curve
       another arm   softly reaching   cuddling
         trees   deer   stars' secrets

the ink slowly dries   cementing herself   on the inkstone
                                      with the self from older times

        a black crescent
on a new sheet of rice paper
                in every tune
                     she utters

(b)

    every month   the sea

               comes & goes   leaving
               a red m
                      o o
                      n

                              on the tree
                           of me
                  somewhere birds
                           are calling

         for the first fruit under the branch
                                    unripe

                                  unborn

            (never ask

                           where it goes)

(c)

rising
     from the left top

                              a swollen
                                    belly

                    from a belly
       a m **oo** n   to be born

                                rising
                                   (as the stroke bends
                                              toward the
earth)

     (d)

                    when you learn 日 you learn 月

                sun & m**oo**n
                      together   they bring light 明
                                                    & tomorrow

you never ask
    the open-end 月
                      what kind of light
                does she invite

        to her
            b **o** dy

(e)
        as I am typing
        y — u — e

    snow comes from the sky
            in silence

                the lost part
                      of me
            sneaks back
                          to remind the rest

    of me
  how I used to
        hold a pen tight
      one stroke
    after another   then the third   the fourth

                or in another life
            how my hands
                    were tattooed

            by ink stains
            that burn
              into

        the black m **oo** n

(f)
    from branch
        to branch
  the m **oo** n follows

                                eyes
                                    tired
                of 0 and 1
                            flickering
                                        on a 13-inch screen
                    even though
            it can reproduce a million m **oo** ns
                                    in a millisecond
                    same shape   size   color

(where is my smiling crescent?)

      (g)

one can write a book about one character, 月, m **oo** n
a typical ideogram, the modern version of 月 comes from its oracle
ancestor, the shape of a waxing crescent. our ancestors were looking at
the same m**oo**n, copied its shape on the tortoise shell. a small curve, a big
curve. everyone who writes has written 月. Li Bai's m**oo**n still shines upon
the bed the window the ground
one can recite a hundred lines that 月 lives in. they are different they are the
same m**oo**n
one, two, three, four. a small curve, a big curve, a short line, another. how
we make m**oo**ns on paper
the many m**oo**ns live inside a body. 脖, neck, 肚, belly, 肘, elbow, 臂, arm,
腕, wrist, 腿, leg, 脚, foot, 肤, skin, 脑, brain, 肝, liver, 肺, lung, 肾, kidney,
脊, spine… in every part of a body lives a m**oo**n
one, two, three, four. a small curve, a big curve, a short line, another. how
we make m**oo**ns and their friends on paper. grind the inkstone, flatten the
paper, dip the brush, count four strokes, make m**oo**ns, before we learn how
to type *y-u-e* on a computer to make a digital m**oo**n
a *yue* rises on the screen, becomes 月
a *yue* rises, grows full, summons the tide. blue tide from the ocean, red tide
from a female body. once a month red tide comes and goes. 月经, moon-
flow. in my body lives
a red m**oo**n
how many red m**oo**ns are there upon the sea
a 月 rises, under its costume, 11100110 10011100 10001000. it's the same
moon it's different than the m**oo**n I made on paper for the first time
for tonight's party, which costume is she going to wear

Justin Kishbaugh

"Three from Three Squared"

I

When, first, time
and second, his mind
lost their rhythm
and blurred their lines,

his ears, like Lear's,
learned to hear
of falsehoods near
and on him played.

His memory, dust,
and the moment never staid.

II

With his mind untethered
and time unhinged,
he shivers in the heat
and sweats in the cold.

His trips to the kitchen increase
as his purpose decreases.

He fills his water and yours

when he remembers

the kitchen is a kitchen,
and the bathroom, a bathroom.

When he forgets,

the kitchen is a bathroom,
and the bathroom, a dream.

III

Like fog-wrapped fuji—

with his hair gone,
            white eyebrows,
and furrowed brow

—he sits and giggles
  in the rain.

His bags so full of memory
he's left them behind.

Tony Lopez

Cartesian Light

At the year's end a comet appeared low in the sky, tail pointing west.
Stroke weights are heavy and only capitals are available.
Lead and other type metals were diverted from their proper use.
You've got to be sensible these days.
A colour looks best when massed and used economically.

In earlier books the initial letters were filled in by hand.
It is a world of propositions that stand in various deductive relations to one another.
This staff does not exist.
Written signs are quotation marks for logical thinking.
Later versions were narrower, with fewer sorts, and required less paper.

The forms are clear and correct and elaborated to the smallest detail.
Bands of men plundered farms for supplies.
Writing enables us to build more content into our beliefs.
The curve and the tail of the lower case 'y' have been altered.
Austerity causes dust to rise.

Fellows and students dispersed into the countryside.
Paper and pencil operations occur in the material world.
For a Cartesian light exists in the air, for a Newtonian it comes from the sun in six and a half minutes.
Use our resources to see if your idea is original.
It wants to be turned around, opened up, and paged through.

Phlogiston is what we now call hydrogen.
The spine-tailed swift flies faster than any other bird (present indicative).
These brackets were made from open-face capital 'O's cut in half.
I come from Colophon, twenty miles northwest of Ephesus.
Alphabetic lines broke through the narrow magical circle.

In the Air

Today, April 17th, there are swallows
and house martins at the beach
just offshore catching flies I can't see
in the air over Maer rocks.
Further out a geared bulk carrier
waiting in the lee of Start Point
is facing west, fixing the horizon.
The sea is relatively calm; it was calm.
It's 4pm as I write this, a kind of preface
to recover a torn seashore poem
washed up here and now.

mudstone crumbs	salt
shell	marsh
fragments	shallow
finest sand	soil
tidal	shingle
grind	marram
every day	grass
every	fescue
night	grass
a medium of	tidal
crawling	path
life	creek
compressed	of
baked,	pollen
lifted	falls
blown away	in whispers

Two large cormorants flew rapidly and very low across the water heading directly towards Langstone Rock, where Dawlish Warren joins the coast just beyond the western edge of the Exe estuary. Their wing tips were almost touching the choppy water. This must have been about 7.45 on Friday morning; I was thirty yards or so out in the sea, only my head visible between the waves that the cormorants flew in among as they powered along one behind the other. I had come down the concrete lifeboat ramp and taken just a few steps on wet sand scattered with various shells, little gleaming stones, and scraps of seaweed, getting quickly into the cool water. The sky was piled up with dark grey cloud overhead but clear and bright at the horizon. The two birds passed close by and continued on their way indifferent to me watching them from the water and they gave no indication if they saw anything unusual.

herring gull	sea lettuce
black-headed gull	arctic tern
mussel	oystercatcher
shell	turnstone
oyster shell	sanderling
clam	carrion crow
shell	jackdaw
cockle shell	pied wagtail
whelk	rock pipit
shell	peregrine
limpet shell	kestrel
winkle	buzzard
shell	brent goose
razor shell	cormorant
crab shell	kingfisher
lobster	farther out
shell	gannet
prawn shell	

A head full of ordinary life
growing and cooking and shopping
then, from wherever, poems come back
stealing away sleep and calm.
A list is a response to what is there —
that knows and owns its sketchiness.
What else? Sea beet, salsify, miner bees,
remember the sudden fall of deep snow
lapwings and golden plovers on the beach
stand out prey for starving peregrines.

I was looking after the three master heading into mist —
a memory I can't quite believe, a ghost ship, no longer there.
Watching from inside the low cloud, depression lifted.

And swimming my slow breast stroke out to the channel I saw a dark-winged butterfly come flying in above the waves, moving with the breeze, heading for the dunes. Was this a migrant painted lady, third generation, from Africa?

Another day, overcast
but with a vertical cone of rays
breaking through a hole in cloud.
The South Hams coast is misty blue
Three container ships wait out on the horizon.
The tideline has been adjusted.
Dogs and their owners run and walk on the beach.
A dozen surfers in shiny neoprene suits
paddle plastic boards into the bay, every so often
one of them peels away and rides a breaking wave
until they fall back into foaming water.

Walking my daily walk, looking at the sea,
thinking of friends now gone, and how we came to be here.

Meaning Empty

In the aleph are two horns of a Semitic steer.
Covers are fed in and drawn around the books.
Cryptographic keys are just special pieces of data.
A phrase of three joined quavers demands sixteen pieces of type for its composition.
Texts are half finished.

Machines write faster than human beings.
England's first paper mill opened at the end of the sixteenth century, on the Deptford River.
The word *cipher* comes from the Arabic *sifr* meaning empty.
Each boundary has to be maintained by constant technological and political management.
Both are material traces of the work in progress.

Deberny types, as well as ornaments, were imported from France.
Almost from the beginning there were no trained workmen available.
A light beam striking the initial cathode causes it to emit electrons.
Many people deny this, mainly out of laziness.
The book was peeled from the forest, and its leaves say what they say.

A puzzle-solving reader is attracted to this borderline.
There seems to be an alternative 'd' with a horizontal serif: the letter is really a reversed 'p'.
Sometimes children unearthed antique coins or remains of a villa.
Get a map from our information desk and start exploring.
Pikemen and musketeers passed through the fields near Woolsthorpe.

Stellar was shelved and Middleton drew Temp, a face much closer to the competition.
Among all these manipulations, none is hard to do except crystallization.
But with notation, progress began to accelerate.
Line-segments could be added and even multiplied.
For example, 'word' is a word, but 'sentence' is not a sentence.

Mary Maxwell

Boudicca in the Underworld

Aeneas could not have observed her on his first visit.
    Dante, of course, also did not see her, although by then
she might be found in the fluttering retinue of Dido
    rather than with Camilla and Penthesilea,
as perhaps the poet would have expected. Boudicca
    floated among those smoldering ghosts whose lives were consumed
by passion's fire; earthbound no longer, the victims of love
    had still not escaped from their suffering. Their own wounded hearts
yet inflamed, Dido and Boudicca languished in tandem
    within death's deep woods, wandered secret alleys enshrouded
with myrtle, or tread sinuous footpaths laid out with all
    the despotic cunning of an imperial gardener.
Why then, it's all true, Aeneas had cried out to Dido,
    that news I heard of your unkind fate! She glowered in anger
as she stood before him half-concealed by leaf-browed shade;
    like the moon, she seemed to him, as it waxes early on
in the month and one sees, or thinks one sees it, between clouds.

    Not long after this Boudicca joined the childless Dido
in death's great estate of mists and starless night. And as
    the moon's mourning visage drifts upon the blue of daylight,
syllables spoken by the British queen pass unnoticed
    as transparent presences in our own keening English.
The Celtic tongue of Boudicca had not been understood
    at first by Romans who came from Latin shores to collect
taxes from local tribes, and even among Hades' rows
    of soldierly cypress, only the ever-courteous
Tristan really followed her words' enigmatic turnings,
    runic and abstract like the decoration of a gold torque
she wore around her neck. In one way or another,
    however, she made her point to the Emperor Nero,
although the Boudiccan revolt ended in defeat.
    This is a woman's resolve. We must conquer or we die,
she chastised the Britons, *and as for you men, you may live*
    and be slaves. Her wild red hair danced to the legions' drumming

as she lay dead in the liberty of her native dirt,
    savage flames darting like the incendiary morris
of burning Londinium mirrored in her cold green eyes.

    That Dante did not notice Boudicca is no surprise,
so captivated as he was by that gentle heart, both
    sweeter-voiced and more familiar, for whom even black winds
fell silent; wings folded, all paused to hear the lovely song
    of Francesca. And though the hero plucked the golden bough
(so like the sacred mistletoe that bears its yellow fruit,
    sown of alien oak, in winter's depths), still Aeneas
does not perceive Boudicca's icy gleam tangled in its
    druidic foliage.

    But she knows him.

    She first heard that story
about the comely widow of Sychaeus as sung by
    an old mercenary who'd spent much time in the bordellos
of Rome. In his version (of which it's said Nero himself
    was inordinately fond) much was made of Dido
and Aeneas making love in a cave, the booms and crashes
    of Virgil's accompanying thunderstorm recreated
by cymbals strategically sounded. And it was from this
    lecherous recension that Boudicca, future widow
of Prasutagus, concluded that any encounter
    between the carnal and the political must be doomed
to end with the violent consequence of a tempest.
    If a woman must decide between one or the other,
she bargained with the mother-goddess Nemetona, *then*
    I'll stay with my children's father, the king. There's just one thing
I ask in return: Don't let me end up like that Dido.

Matz McLaughlin

Après Villon

"En cheminant sans croix ne pille"*
I brought my soul bare to these hills

"Je suys pecheur, je le scay bien"
We drag our sins to Lethe then

"Les mons ne bougent de leurs lieux"
I've come to pray, to make anew

"Oy, ou tout vif aller es cieulx"
Knelt in the dawn, the streams my pews

"Que ma povre priere ait lieu"
Many forsaken, heard the few

"Je vous diray: J'ay tort et honte"
Humble, reborn, penance I want

"Povrete tous nous suit et trace"
And death swoops down, gold turns to dust

"Telle qu'il pert vent et alaine"
Nailed to the wheel, to spin again

"Autant en emporte ly vens"
Rides the tail of the wind my song

---

*All of the quotations in this poem were taken from the volume The Retrospect of François Villon (Oxford University Press, 1924).

Three Seasons Haiku

The crimson leaves cling
Under the snow-dusted road
The promise of spring

Old Panther

(for Ezra Pound)

War on all fronts
Confusion reigns all around
What's this sense of panic I hear
That runs through the town?

Old Panther
No longer locked in a cage
I stop and often wonder
What you would think
Of this day and age

The people need poetry
Truth to disinfect all the lies
That run to our fingertips
And fill up our eyes

Old Panther
No longer locked in a cage
I stop and often wonder
What you would think
Of this day and age

Jesus Christ himself
Will not bother to come back
We are all far beyond help
On this dark-fated track

Old Panther
No longer locked in a cage
I stop and often wonder
What you would think
Of this day and age

When our greed expires
And the tide resigns from the shore
Let's relight the fires
And rid us of the devil's whore

Old Panther
No longer locked in a cage
I stop and often wonder
What you would think
Of this day and age

Biljana D. Obradović

Lost Loot Value

Hiroshima vases found
by an American soldier
after the explosion

brought proudly to the show by a son
whose father, an American soldier, saved
this war loot from World War II,

now wants the appraiser to put
a monetary value,
on this antique

on *Antiques Roadshow,*
and the appraiser says
$2-3,000

adding that museums would
want these types of objects
to tell the story

of how very few things
survived the nuclear blast,
how every thing,

people, Japanese mothers,
daughters, sons, grandparents…all
turned into ash in a second.

My Yoga Class

for Laura Flora, my yogini

Laura starts by giving out Mexican blankets to sit on,
then purple blocks and belts, as we unroll our mats, remove
our watches, place our water bottles like talismans on the ground.

When all sixteen women (with occasional men)
are cross-legged, she begins. Her theme today,
"What are we thankful for, or should be?"

This for November, the Thanksgiving month.
So each day she tells people what she's thankful for
—for simple things, food on the table, shelter,

electricity, or water, for the people around us each day.
I half-listen. I don't like sermons. I don't want to be in church.
I don't want someone tell me what to do.

While she speaks, I have to move my legs, already achy
from this pose on the mat (and we haven't even started yet!).
Even with the blanket underneath for support, my sacrum

(which she has realigned herself so many times) hurts.
I am afraid to ask her to do it again as she always comments,
if she were a chiropractor, she would have been rich.

She has given me names of chiropractors, but I don't call them.
After three rounds of Om, listening to each other breathing
we begin with increasing intensity: from child to down dog

to warrior, to pigeon, to whatever end pose she has devised
for the part of the body we're concentrating on today—the core?
After an hour or more, another quiet rest on our backs, *shavasana*—

which she breaks with a ceremonial ringing of small bells—
we say Om once more then quit, and I drag myself past
people meditating over Bloody Marys at the Ruby Slipper.

Symmetry

We arrive at the train station, excited
about our return to Venezia,
but instead, after the short walk, are startled.
At Hotel Basilea, the desk clerk Marco
tells us what seems nobody's business,
chatting with my husband and me.
Two summers have passed since
he's seen us. For fifteen years
we've come every or every other year,
regulars enough to confide in us.
He says that his love life is so bad
even if he threw himself off
the Rialto Bridge, no one would care.

The glass chandelier on our large
palazzo-like room's ceiling is asymmetrical:
five balls of light, but between
two of them there is too much space,
more than between the other lights.
We are used to the spaces between balls
being exactly the same.
At this, not a mass-produced chandelier—
a beautiful, expensive, hand blown,
a Murano glass piece, with brown and
light yellow, almost gold-colored glass,
and ornamental leaves and flowers,
we cannot stop looking.

My husband and I wonder, what if someone
were to knock it with a long umbrella,
break it accidentally? We won't.
We are careful, but also obsessed.
It bothers us. Why did the artist
make it asymmetrical? For what purpose?
A mistake? We yearn for symmetry.
We look up, like Marco not being in love—
surprised when we lack love, we suffer,
we crave, and repeat odd things helplessly.

The Mask: Il Dottore, Il Medico Della Peste

I. Venice, Italy, 1998

The beaklike, bespectacled, papier-mâché,
white and black mask I brought on the plane
from Venice across the pond
has been collecting dust, hanging
on our living room wall for years.
I bought the traditional mask of the plague-

doctor found at a specialized *Carnivale* store.
Venice, the city where my husband
and I have been going each summer;
it has a special place in our hearts.
But instead of proposing in an osteria in Venice,
when the time came, when it was necessary

(we'd been trying to get pregnant and I did),
he proposed at Venezia, a pizza and pasta
place, in Mid-City, New Orleans,
where people also wear masks
to celebrate Mardi Gras. But, in Venice
he never wanted to ride in a gondola

until I managed to persuade him at last;
two years later, the gondola ride happened.
It was far too expensive to ride on our own.
So, we went with his students, a couple,
and our two-year-old baby son—
not very romantic—neither were

the arias the gondolier sang, too touristy,
yet going down narrow canals at sunset
with the red and yellow sun reflecting
against the palazzo, still seemed magical,
so that one would have wanted to kiss.
Alas, we didn't. Maybe he was too shy

(needed a mask!), in front of his students.
The next summer on the way to the airport in a
water taxi, predawn, the light was beautiful,
then the sky opened, the pelting rain kissed my cheeks,
lightning nearly struck the boat so it almost capsized;
we nearly lost our baby, the stroller, all sixteen suitcases.

II. Covid-19, New Orleans, 2020

I never imagined we'd need this mask.
Suddenly, during the Covid epidemic,
we had to wear masks, not for romance
but to protect ourselves from the invisible.
The old plague-doctor mask reminded me of what
my parents had brought from India, peacock

feathers, beautiful—green and purple—sign
of good fortune. But someone said no,
remove them because they bring bad luck.
(My parents both died of cancer.) What
should we do with romance, destroy it?
The ancient ones knew the value of masks,

protection from bad smells, from plague,
death, sorrow, *dottores* donning masks with
lavender (sweet smelling), roses, carnations, herbs.
They wore gloves, boots, drooping black capes
and wide-brimmed hats. Only with wooden
canes did they take off clothes, touching bodies

with the end of their long sticks.
In 1656 half a million people in Rome,
in Naples died. Those left behind, terrified
by doctors in costume and dying loved ones,
understood how beauty and fear married
in masks, so saved them to save the future.

Our masks did not save millions. Covid
killed them, but when putting on
the plague-doctor mask or Covid mask,
we think of half-faces looking at us.
Doctors don clear plastic shield-masks, and
we see again how easily horror comes.

We have nightmares of peacock feathers
and lavender. We try to talk as we once did,
lovingly,-but some words get broken,
some are buried. Still with masks on
(although some are saying, "Take them off!"),
we go on, while mask stares at us from the wall.

A Greek Island Vacation

for my brother, Bata

I.
By Ipsos town on Corfu, the sea is clear
clean, an aqua temple for tourists ready
for rest, for swimming, for eating *souvlaki*.

New patrons arrive each Saturday by ferry from
the east, the Greek mainland, or the west, Italy.
As they walk this ground, do they understand

Odysseus may have stepped where they step.
They swim, tan, eat some octopus or a gyro wrap,
then drink Ouzo. When they tire of the sea,

they go into Kerkyra, to shoe shop
just because...or wander through Orthodox churches,
or take a tour of the forts, old and new,

one built by Venetians, the other by Englishmen.
They gaze where the Durrell brothers played and wrote
travel pieces, with lots of male cicadas chirping,

attracting the female ones to mate, *tzitzikas*.
Now I hear them at night, all the time, everywhere,
their music making you hungry, waking you up.

Some introspective types, even take a drive
uphill for a tour of Achilleion Palace, beyond the blue
water where infinity starts, but they love most

the villa owned by much beloved Elizabeth, Austro-
Hungarian queen. Imagine the elaborate balls
held there, unseen by the island below.

II.
I take my son on a small boat ride across
from the main city, to the island of Vido, to see
where a hundred years ago Serbian soldiers

debarked, fleeing the German army,
walking for weeks with torn shoes or barefoot,
starving, in the middle of winter through snow.

After contracting typhoid, they landed on Ipsos
where we have come to swim. Thousands got sick,
and died on this desolate island, once a hospital,

now a tomb with their names lined up, divisions
identified, their home towns. We start to search
for a granduncle who may have died here

long ago. But now time is short. We remember,
and cruise to see other little towns, dive through caves,
buy local olive carvings, kumquat liquor, candies,

jam this land sweetens, obligatory souvenirs, then escape
to our lives wanting it all, hands, heads with new perspectives,
but we never find my granduncle's name.

KENJI MIYAZAWA (1896-1933)
TRANSLATED BY HIDETOSHI TOMIYAMA AND MICHAEL PRONKO

The Spirit Song

The sun reigns, the splendor
Pouring down a platinum rain
As we bend over the black dirt
Sowing seeds of the grass of truth.

The sun reigns in the vault
Brimming, spanning blue light,
Light's sweat, as we sense
No blemish to the ends of the atmosphere.

The sun reigns, the glass window
Is pellucid and calm,
Yet we, searching for truth,
Must bathe in a chalk-white fog.

The sun reigns, in splendor
The Solar System at high noon,
In the course of steep journeys,
We shall tread the steps of light.

Untitled

My chest is now
A saline lake, hot and sad,
Along two hundred miles of the shore,
Forests of coal-black lepidodendrons continue,
And do I have to,
Until reptile turns into bird,
Motionless,
Lie down here?

Untitled

Fever, gasps, losing the real
On the border of dying, dozing
All night, through the day
Thou this way hast guarded me

Without ornaments, without shoes
In sackcloth, ash-colored
Assuming the habit of humble ones
Thou residest with a calm heart

Awesome it is to know thy name,
Yet it seems right to surmise
Thou art the goddess supreme,
The one recorded thrice in the Book.

Hence, at the time of agony, and fever
Of a mind confused, disarrayed,
Thou camest not by the name of a god
But by Dharma's precious Name

Without ornaments, without shoes,
For the offspring of endless Karma
With clouds of sorrow on thy brow,
Thou residest serene.

Stephen Romer

A Set of Satirical Verses

(in honour of EP)

Ageing starts

when you're a stranger in your culture
ends when you're a stranger in your chair.

On Hearing that Keats & Wordsworth have Trigger Warnings:

Beware, O reader, do—
this poem has palpable designs on *you!*

Considerate Construction

In Oxford, even the building sites
preach at one today:
their billboards proclaim,
For the first time,
This department will really be
Open to Everyone!
Everyone?
Hmmm, notes the infected tomcat
slinking past, ready to spray.

There's no escape. I turn to glimpse
a white van from the Council tootling by:
Doing Good
it announces, on its filthy side.

Neurodiverse

The excitable press officer
is 'beyond excited'
to be trumpeting another
'brand new poet':

«She is half-deaf, half-Danish»
which is also,
let us own it,
'beyond niche'.

His Beloved announces she has found a Dance Class

The way we danced till three
the soft shoe whisper
piano and drum brush
in Chet's
Everything Happens to Me

the slightest shift
in tempo
and you're dancing away
being danced
to the heart of love

away from me
and I can only watch
you cheek to cheek in heaven,
streaming and entranced
in my diminished seven.

Pozzo Revisited
(*verses in praise of envy and rage*)

The Lobb boots are up a niche
I notice, the bike is now a Ridgeway,
top of the range,
'not just any piece of shit'.

He asks me to guard it,
so I leave it unlocked by the skip.
His difficult second novel
wins a prize for the 'difficult second novel'.
Whole swathes of the *LRB*
are given over to his poems
—I'm finding it hard to breathe—
—they've never noticed me—

and he's very nearly scraped
a top professorship.
Pozzo's on a roll. Anything else?
I'll credit him though with this—it's a brilliant
Chair of Faculty who coolly
reels off with humour:

Chairman's Business? None.
Any Other Business? None.
Matters Arising? None.

Du Bellay, 21st century style

When you are sad, and imminently grey,
Will you take down my poems and say
That bastard took and took and took
From me, for the sake of his lousy book'
—And have me, who am truly old and grey
Terribly in handcuffs taken away?

Pension Time!

Scrutinizing my pension claim
the French bureaucracy
detects *aucune anomalie*
in my *parcours*
which means I'm squeaky clean
even for them…

No anomalies — and all those years—
dear god, please,
find me some anomalies
and remove this dreadful badge of shame!

Two Clerihew (and a Mauberley)

Playing Patience, **T.S. Eliot** once said,
He enjoyed: it was close to being dead.
There are others who prefer the Hypnosis
Of writing Clerihew, to weather the Kenosis.

Ted Hughes went full thrott-
Le
And compared **T.S.Eliot**
To an axolot-
L.

Mr Eliot kept asking, out of spite,
'What does **Mr Pound** believe?' till Ezra shot back to Blighty
1) *The Criterion is Shite.*
2) *Aphrodite.*

My Bookends

Sporadically, a name appears
In the bookshop's meagre poetry section,
Between Lord Rochester and Christina Rossetti.
But ephemeral, like malaria or the dengue,
—Unlike Christina and his Lordship's erection—
It vanishes again for years.

Ron Smith

ALBUM

1
1910

Profile, right to left, mouth tight,
brows seemingly knit, hair—O the hair!
A box of locks, lush, fluffed vertical,
the full ear showing, eyes sternly regarding
the past (if our left is the past), brocaded coat,
white collar flaring . . .

2
Dorothy's Man, c. 1911

She smiles at him, genuinely,
let's say, and he leans his head
toward her, Mephistophelian smile,
even a pointed heard. Her hands, his hands
each in its own pocket. A space between them.

She's a not-precisely demure maid; he's
presented as a rake, mesmerizing her
with his eyes, hair a roiling cloud quite
in contrast to her smooth pull-back into
a generous bun.

3
1918: *Pavannes and Divisions*

The poet lounges in a chair, legs crossed,
left hand loose like dying blossoms,
wool-wrapped as if cold, staring now
(and yet again) to the camera's left,
now as if facing a high wind, sideburn
anchoring the billowing hair. The nod
to Whistler's Thomas Carlyle is instructive,

the older image rendered staid by this
action-in-repose, this diagonal slash
of Modernism . . .

4
Passport: July 1919

Below the graceful calligraphy
of his signature, below the brutal
"ANNULE" of "PARIS, FRANCE"
Citizen Pound looks prosperous,
hair rich but under control, eyes
unromantic, gazing only slightly to
the camera's right. Oh, dear, there remains
the unruly collar, and the necktie's off-
kilter twist. But, the full face is solid,
mustache respectable, coat, overcoat
capable of keeping a gentleman warm
anywhere in this world. But it's July . . .

5
1920

. . . then there's this
skeptical downward
sideye, this bohemian
sneer, this not-quite-direct
stare, contemptuous toss
of turbulent hair merging
with the background darkness . . .

6
Pound's Rooms, Paris, 1923

He's the center of attention, drawing Ford's,
Joyce's disapproving eyes to his rude
chair slouch, his rumpled irritability.
Above him, the only one not seated,
lawyer John Quinn pushes back his coat,
stares straight into us as if to say, This

is actually none of your business. (Is that
a Picasso on the wall behind him?)

7
1 May 1940, Photo by Carl Mydans

The aging man looking up from the black
typewriter, seeming to reach for something
in his right pocket, flings a suspicious glare
at Mydans—who will publish this in *Life*
with the caption "Journalist and writer
Ezra Pound, composing profascist
commentaries on stationery emblazoned
with Mussolini's motto . . ." No "poet."

8
Five Days after Admission to St. Elizabeth's

None of us will forget those pleading eyes.

Hair buzzed severely over the ears,
though still vigorous on top—above a
corrugated forehead, a fan of
exclamation marks over the left eyebrow.
He yet has only a few wrinkles below or
beside those eyes. Look away for a moment . . .

Now: His mouth is slightly open—imagine it
trembling. How can his necktie be reasonably
straight? Of course, that stubborn right collar,
shrunken by forties fashion, sticks out over the
sport coat. Head cocked slightly to our left,
the poet's in shallow focus against an utterly
blank background.

9
Washington, 18 April 1958: Free

Outside the Federal Courthouse,
narrowed eyes more crafty than angry,

his mouth twists with irony. A big black hat,
a ropy, old man's neck. He's on his way
to Richmond, Virginia. But he won't be there
long. The old world has claimed him.
He needs to go "home."

10
Naples, 9 July 1958

There it is, the fascist salute
from the *Cristoforo Colombo*.
The poet looks more happy than defiant,
showing more teeth than I've ever seen.

His belt's too long, lolling out
a good four inches, both armpits dark
with sweat. Summer whites. Hair, beard
white. But his face now is young.

Look at the extended hand, the unbent elbow.
He knows how to give the salute properly.
He wants to get it right.

11
Venice, 1964

Here's the crafty old coot
in a fine-looking hat, nearly
a cowboy hat. Black. He
looks old, doesn't he? But aware
as well as wary?

Head turned slightly away, but
eyes on the camera. He is not
posing as he did so often when he
was young. He is watching us
watching him.

12
1970

By Gawd, here's the old boy in motion,
an action hero climbing some serious stairs,
coat impeccably buttoned where it should be,
hair a flattened halo of froth, cane down and
doing its job. He looks ready for a fight.
Maybe with an editor.

13
1971, with Olga Rudge

That's a look every human being wants
to have, to give. Near tears, or beyond,
utterly devoted—each to the other.

Their lips open just a little. Her unseen hand
is under his coat, tenderly on his shoulder
or neck. They look deeply into each others' eyes.

Behind them, between them, is a vehicle,
maybe a station wagon. One of them is leaving.
One of them.

14
E Morto Ezra Pound

a black gondola
heavy with poetry rowed
by four hard working men

15
EZRA POUND

I have seen that simple stone,
pale but not perfectly white.

Some ten of us stood around,
silent, looking forward to the night,

dinner nearly always to die for,
but never ready till long past daylight.

We were there to study his work,
shrunk now to three syllables. "Cretic." "Right."

Contributors

Mary de Rachewiltz, who grew up in Gais, Pustertal, in Sudtirol, Italy, is the daughter of Ezra Pound and violinist Olga Rudge. Her internationally acclaimed memoir *Discretions: Ezra Pound: Father and Teacher* (1971) chronicles her life up to Pound's return to Italy in 1958. Among her prolific body of work are her Italian translations of a selection of Poundian texts, *Opere scelte* (Mondadori, 1970) and a complete English/Italian edition of *The Cantos* (Mondadori, 1985). With A. David Moody and Joanna Moody, she edited *Ezra Pound to His Parents: Letters 1895–1929* (Oxford, 2011). Apart from her archival work at the Beinecke Library at Yale, co-organizing exhibitions on Pound, maintaining the Pound archive at her home, Brunnenburg, Merano, Italy, writing essays, and lecturing on her father's work around the world, she has also been a working poet all her life, with poems in Italian and English. Her work has also been translated into multiple languages. Her poetry collections in English include *Family Tree, Whose World? Selected Poems, For the Wrong Reason,* and *Fifteen Poems* (Ed. Ted Wojtasik). In 2024 Bertoni Editore published *Processo in verso: Tutte le poesie italiane,* de Rachewiltz's complete poems composed in Italian.

Silvia Falsaperla is a graduate of University of Toronto. She has published poetry and prose in Canadian and American literary journals and anthologies. She has been a winner of literary contests in Canada, read her work in international literary conferences, and her poems have been translated into Italian, Spanish, and Japanese. Her hybrid collection of poetry and short stories entitled *The Garden of Kolymbethra and Other Poems and Stories about Sicily* was published in 2024 by Legas. and a new collection of poetry is forthcoming with Ekstasis Editions. She loves dogs, to travel, and ride her bike.

Rhett Forman lives on the staked plains of Texas where he is Assiatant Professor at Tarleton State Univeristy. He is a 2025 Best of the Net, Pushcart Prize, and Best New Poets nominee. His poetry, scholarship, and translations have most recently appeared in *Apple Valley Review, Spoon River Poetry Review, West Branch, Midwest Quarterly, Ezra Pound and the Spanish World* (Clemson), and *T. S. Eliot: The Rose Garden and After* (Routledge).

John Gery's seven books of poetry include *The Enemies of Leisure, A Gallery of Ghosts, Have at You Now!,* and *Davenport's Version,* a narrative poem set in Civil War New Orleans. He has received fellowships from the NEA, the Fulbright Foundation, and the University of Minnesota Institute for Advanced Study, among others. As a critic, he has written extensively about modernist and contemporary poetry, including his book, *Nuclear Annihilation and Contemporary Poetry: Ways of Nothingness* as well as many essays on Pound. A Research Professor of English at the University of New Orleans, he directs the Ezra Pound Center for Literature and is Series Editor of the EPCL Book Series at Clemson University Press. Recent co-edited books include *Cross-Cultural Ezra Pound, Ezra Pound and the Spanish World,* and the English-Spanish poetry anthology, *"Song Up Out of Spain."*

Jeff Grieneisen is the author of two books of poetry: *Good Sumacs* (MAMMOTH Books 2010) and *The Language of Phosphorescence* (Lavender Ink 2024). He is a professor of literature and creative writing at State College of Florida and part time professor of writing and literature at Ringling College of Art and Design. He acts as liaison between the Ezra Pound Society and Northeast Modern Language Association and serves as president of The Imagist Society (imagistsociety.org).

Chengru He 何琤茹 is the author of a hybrid collection *I Would Vanish into Its Stronger Existence* (Wet Cement 2024) and a book of poems *M O月 N* (Parlor Press/Free Verse Edition 2025); the Chinese translator of two books and a few chapbook projects. Her writing, translation, and multi-media works appear in *Ancient Exchange, Colorado Review, Fence, Gulf Coast, The Kenyon Review,* among others. She is currently based in Salt Lake City, where she is a PhD candidate in English Literature and Creative Writing at the University of Utah.

Justin Kishbaugh directs the Writing Center and is the Associate Director of Academic Success and a Professor of Writing at Roger Williams University School of Law. He holds an M.F.A. in Creative Writing from the Jack Kerouac School of Disembodied Poetics at Naropa University and a Ph.D. in English Literature from Duquesne University. Justin has co-edited and appeared in previous volumes of this anthology series, and his recent scholarship uses Modernist poetics to promote equity in legal writing. Those titles include, "'No Ideas but in Things': Rubrics, First-Generation Students, and the Concretizing of Abstract Standards" (2023); "'Go in Fear of Abstractions': Precision, Pronouns, and Power in Legal Writing," (2024);

and "Gut Renovations, Rubrics, and the Reduction of Bias in Standard Edited American English and Legal Writing" (2024). He also has the chapter "'Now Sun Rises in Ram Sign' and 'Addendum for C'" forthcoming in *Readings in the Cantos: Volume III* and dreams of one day working at Trader Joe's. He supports the Aston Villa Football Club and is particularly fond of negronis, gyros, and the Rolling Stones.

Tony Lopez is best known for his book *False Memory*, published in USA by The Figures and in UK by Shearsman. His poetry features in *Twentieth-Century British and Irish Poetry* (Oxford), *The New Concrete* (Hayward), *The Dark Would* (Apple Pie), *The Art of the Sonnet* (Harvard), *The Reality Street Book of Sonnets* (RSE), *Other: British and Irish Poetry since 1970* (Wesleyan) and *Conductors of Chaos* (Picador). He has received awards from Arts Council England, the Society of Authors, and the Arts and Humanities Research Council. Recent poems have been published in *Poetry*, *Blackbox Manifold* and *The Stinging Fly*. Originally from Brixton in South London, he taught for many years at Plymouth University and now lives on the Devon coast

Mary Maxwell is the author of five volumes of poems, *An Imaginary Hellas*, *Emporia*, *Cultural Tourism*, *Nine Over Sixes* and *Oral Lake*, as well as the digital/audio chapbook, *Trail* (all published by LongNookBooks). Her first-book manuscript was a finalist for numerous competitions, including the National Poetry Series, the Walt Whitman Award and the Yale Younger Poets Prize. Individual poems originally appeared in *Agni*, *The Nation*, *The New Republic*, *Paris Review*, *Provincetown Arts*, *Salmagundi*, *Southern Review*, *Slate* and *Yale Review*. As an independent scholar, Mary has published her essays and reviews in literary periodicals such as *Arion*, *Boston Review*, *Literary Matters*, *On the Seawall*, *Partisan Review* and *Threepenny Review*. Ongoing prose projects include a series of essays on Ford Madox Ford and American poetry, and on the poet and dance critic Edwin Denby. She will also be contributing to the forthcoming *Routledge Companion to Ezra Pound*.

Matz McLaughlin is a junior associate professor at Tokyo University of Science. His research focuses on 20th century poetry, including the writings of Ezra Pound, but more specifically, the Beat Generation poets who write about ecological and environmental issues. He is the author of several articles on Beat generation poets and is currently conducting doctoral research on vanished Beat poet Lew Welch at Université Libre de Bruxelles (ULB).

Kenji Miyazawa (1896-1933) lived in Hanamaki, a town in the northern Honshu Island of Japan. The eldest son of a wealthy, devout Buddhist merchant, he taught at a local agricultural school and then tried to help improve the condition of nearby poor villages, providing lectures, cultural activities, and fertilization plans. However, he prematurely died of tuberculosis. In his lifetime he published only two books (one of poems and another of stories in 1924), though his literary genius was apparent. Soon after his death, works from his manuscripts started to be published; since then, he has been among the most widely read and discussed modern authors. His kaleidoscopic tales and fables evade expectations about the genre of children's stories. From early tanka poems (5-7-5-7-7 syllables) through free verse works (sometimes hundreds of lines long) to later stanzaic poems in traditional meters (the 7-5 or 5-7 syllable pattern), his poetry exhibits thematic variety and formal inventiveness. His themes include communion with nature, elegies for his deceased sister, compassion for the fate of common people, and extreme visionary and religious experiences. The poems are often composed of subtly modulated verbal passages interacting in multivocal dialogism.

Biljana D. Obradović, a Serbian-American poet/translator, Professor of English at Xavier University of Louisiana, New Orleans, has published: four collections of poems, most recently *Little Disruptions* (WordTech, 2022); seven translations of poetry collections and Dubravka Djurić's *The Politics of Hope (After the War)* (Roof Books, 2023); two anthologies of poems as editor and translator, including *Cat Painters: An Anthology of Contemporary Serbian Poetry*, Dialogos, 2016, Serbian *Atlanta Review* (2021), as well as Philip Dacey's *Heavenly Muse: Essays on Poetry* (Dialogos, 2020). Her fifth collection of poems, *Called by Distances*, is coming out in March 2026 from LSU Press.

Michael Pronko is Professor of American Literature at Meiji Gakuin University, Tokyo. He teaches seminars in novel-to-film adaptation and American culture. His publications include a chapter on Japanese jazz for the *Routledge Companion to Jazz Studies*, a textbook of his essays, *Inbound/Outbound Japan*, and numerous articles for magazines and newspapers. He's also a novelist (the Detective Hiroshi series) and runs the website, *Jazz in Japan*.

Stephen Romer is a poet, anthologist, critic and translator. His latest collection is *Set Thy Love in Order: New & Selected Poems* (2017). *Le fauteuil jaune*, a bi-lingual selection with French translations appeared in 2021. His book of critical essays, including essays on Pound, *Chaos and the Clean Line: Writings on Franco-British Modernism* was published in 2024. He is Lecturer in French at Brasenose College, Oxford.

Ron Smith was in the very first group of scholars to study at the Ezra Pound Center for Literature at Brunnenburg. Poet Laureate of Virginia 2014-2016, he has published four volumes of poetry with Louisiana State University Press, most recently *That Beauty in the Trees*. His *Running Again in Hollywood Cemetery*, judged "a close runner-up" for the National Poetry Series Open Competition by Margaret Atwood, was published first by University Presses of Florida and reissued 2020 in an enhanced edition by MadHat Press. Smith's poems have appeared in numerous periodicals and dozens of anthologies, including *The Nation, Kenyon Review, Georgia Review, Plume*, and *Arts of War & Peace* (Université Paris Diderot). Winner of *Southern Poetry Review*'s Guy Owen Prize, Smith has presented his poems about George Washington and Thomas Jefferson at Mount Vernon and Monticello, has read poems about Virginia's history and landscapes on the floor of the Virginia House of Delegates and the Virginia Senate, his Italy-inspired poems at the Keats-Shelley House and the American Ambassador's Official Residence in Rome, as well as his poems about modernists to Hemingway scholars at the American Library in Paris and on the Eiffel Tower.

Hidetoshi Tomiyama is Professor Emeritus of Meiji Gakuin University, Tokyo. His collection of essays *Hiyu To Hango: Amerika No Shi To Hihyo* (in Japanese, meaning *Metaphor and Irony: American Poetry and Criticism*) was issued in 2023. His translations into Japanese include Walt Whitman's *Leaves of Grass: The First Edition*, William Carlos Williams' *In the American Grain*, and Hugh Kenner's *The Stoic Comedians*.

www.ingramcontent.com/pod-product-compliance
Lightning Source LLC
Chambersburg PA
CBHW061605110426
42742CB00039B/2853